FOAL

The Story of Our Holidays
KWANZAA

Joanna Ponto and Carol Gnojewski

Enslow Publishing
101 W. 23rd Street
Suite 240
New York, NY 10011
USA
enslow.com

Published in 2017 by Enslow Publishing, LLC.
101 W. 23rd Street, Suite 240, New York, NY 10011

Copyright © 2017 by Carol Gnojewski
Additional materials copyright © 2017 by Enslow Publishing, LLC.

All rights reserved.

No part of this book may be reproduced by any means without the written permission of the publisher.

Library of Congress Cataloging-in-Publication Data
Names: Ponto, Joanna, author. | Gnojewski, Carol, author.
Title: Kwanzaa / Joanna Ponto and Carol Gnojewski.
Description: New York, NY : Enslow Publishing, [2017] | Series: The story of our holidays | Includes bibliographical references and index. | Audience: Grades 4-6.
Identifiers: LCCN 2016001035| ISBN 9780766076235 (library bound) | ISBN 9780766076211 (pbk.) | ISBN 9780766076228 (6-pack)
Subjects: LCSH: Kwanzaa--Juvenile literature.
Classification: LCC GT4403 .P65 2016 | DDC 394.2612--dc23
LC record available at http://lccn.loc.gov/2016001035

Printed in the United States of America

To Our Readers: We have done our best to make sure all website addresses in this book were active and appropriate when we went to press. However, the author and the publisher have no control over and assume no liability for the material available on those websites or on any websites they may link to. Any comments or suggestions can be sent by e-mail to customerservice@enslow.com.

Portions of this book originally appeared in the book *Kwanzaa: Seven Days of African-American Pride* by Carol Gnojewski

Photos Credits: Cover, p. 1 Stockbyte/Getty Images; p. 4 Jupiterimages/liquidlibrary/Thinkstock; p. 6 Hill Street Studios/Blend Images/Getty Images; p. 8 Malcolm Ali/WireImage/Getty Images; p. 9 William Lovelace/Express/Getty Images; p. 12 Kayte Deioma/Alamy; p. 14 Timothy R. Nichols/Shutterstock.com; p. 15 Education Images/UIG/Getty Images; p. 18 The Washington Post/Getty Images; p. 20 Jon-Michael Sullivan/The Augusta Chronicle/ZUMA Press; p. 23 Fanfo/Shutterstock.com; p. 24 Photo Researchers/Science Source/Getty Images; p. 26 Kathryn Scott Osler/The Denver Post/Getty Images; p. 29 Cheryl Wells.

Contents

Chapter 1
　　Heri za Kwanzaa! 5

Chapter 2
　　What Is Kwanzaa? 7

Chapter 3
　　Teachings and Symbols 10

Chapter 4
　　The Seven Days of Kwanzaa 16

Chapter 5
　　Celebrate Kwanzaa 25

　　Kwanzaa Craft 28
　　Glossary 30
　　Learn More 31
　　Index 32

Kwanzaa is a time for Americans of African heritage to celebrate with family and friends.

Chapter 1

Heri za Kwanzaa!

For more than 20 million people of African heritage in the United States, December 26 marks the beginning of the festivities that last until the New Year. It is the start of a seven-day African American harvest festival called Kwanzaa. During Kwanzaa, many African Americans practice the traditions of their ancestors far away in the Southern Hemisphere on the continent of Africa.

Like Christmas, Kwanzaa is a time of gathering and of giving gifts. But Kwanzaa does not take the place of Christmas.

Although it is a relatively new holiday, Kwanzaa includes a variety of customs and traditions. These are ways African Americans can celebrate their African roots and ancestry.

During Kwanzaa, African Americans celebrate all that they have in common with each other and with the people of Africa. Homes are decorated in bright African colors of black, red, and green. African clothing and hairstyles are worn. People greet each other in Swahili, a language spoken in most parts of Africa. *"Heri za Kwanzaa!"* they say. That means Happy Kwanzaa!

The Kwanzaa Flag

The black, red, and green bendera (ban-DAY-rah) is the Kwanzaa flag. It is based on the flag created by Marcus Garvey, a black leader. The colors of the flag have a special meaning. Black stands for the people. Red stands for struggle. Green stands for future hopes. The flag is hung with the black stripe on top to show that people come first.

Chapter 2

What Is Kwanzaa?

Kwanzaa is the first African American holiday. To highlight that achievement, the holiday is named for the Swahili word *kwanza*, meaning "first."

An African American teacher named Dr. Maulana Karenga created the holiday. He pieced together old and new rituals from Africa and the United States.

A Thanksgiving for the Inside

The Swahili phrase *matunda ya kwanza* means "first fruits." In Africa, first fruits refer to crops of food that are gathered or harvested at the end of the growing season. A first fruits harvest festival honors the land and all that grows each year. It brings people together to celebrate shared bonds of family and life.

Kwanzaa is about the gathering of people. African Americans come together to grow on the inside by learning, sharing, and remembering past achievements. Dr. Karenga and his friends held the first Kwanzaa celebration in 1966 in California.

In planning a new holiday, Dr. Karenga had to answer many tough questions. When would Kwanzaa be held? How many days would it last? Who would the holiday be for? How would people celebrate it? Dr. Karenga made these decisions and wrote them down carefully so others could follow his guidelines.

Creating Kwanzaa was Dr. Karenga's way of helping African Americans understand their rich history and culture. He wanted them to see their lives from an African point of view.

Dr. Maulana Karenga, a professor of African studies, created Kwanzaa. The holiday has become very popular in the United States.

Civil rights leaders like Martin Luther King Jr. fought for equal rights for African Americans.

African American History

African Americans have had a complicated history ever since they were brought to America to be slaves. For many years, they were denied the rights that white people enjoyed. But in the 1960s, many positive changes happened quickly in the black community. Because of the work of civil rights leaders, African Americans gained new freedoms.

Black and white people now have equal rights, but some African Americans wanted an identity apart from white America. They wanted the power to make the laws for their own communities. Others wanted to form their own nation. But mostly, African Americans wanted to remember their history and respect their African roots. Dr. Karenga created Kwanzaa so people would have a holiday that pays tribute to the African American culture and identity.

Chapter 3

Teachings and Symbols

Dr. Karenga wanted black people to honor their roots in Africa. There were strong traditions there that had been lost in America. But he also didn't want them to forget how far they had come. He believed they should take control of their lives and their communities.

To build a stronger future, he knew that African Americans had to rethink who they were and what they wanted to be. Did they think of themselves as former slaves? Did they think of themselves as minority Americans? Did they think of themselves as a part of the African world?

The Seven Principles

In his own life, Dr. Karenga decided that "the first step forward is a step backward to Africa and African roots." He began to study African history. He traveled to many African countries and talked to people there. He learned how they lived and what was important in their lives. The wisdom he gathered became the Nguzo Saba.

The Nguzo Saba is a list of seven principles, or teachings, that African Americans celebrate during Kwanzaa. There are seven principles for the seven days of Kwanzaa:

- Day 1 *Umoja*: unity
- Day 2 *Kujichagulia*: self-determination
- Day 3 *Ujima*: collective work and responsibility
- Day 4 *Ujamaa*: cooperative economics
- Day 5 *Nia*: purpose
- Day 6 *Kuumba*: creativity
- Day 7 *Imani*: faith

The Importance of Seven

Seven is an important number during Kwanzaa. An extra "a" in the Swahili word *kwanza* gives the holiday's name seven letters. As you read this book, look for things that come in groups of seven.

Setting Up

Would you like to make a Kwanzaa display? Here is what to do. First, find a mat. It can be a placemat, a tablecloth, or a piece of African cloth. Place your mat in the center of a table. The mat will make a foundation. All the other symbols will rest on it.

Next, add some fruits and vegetables. Put them in a basket or bowl. Or set them directly on the mat. The fruits and

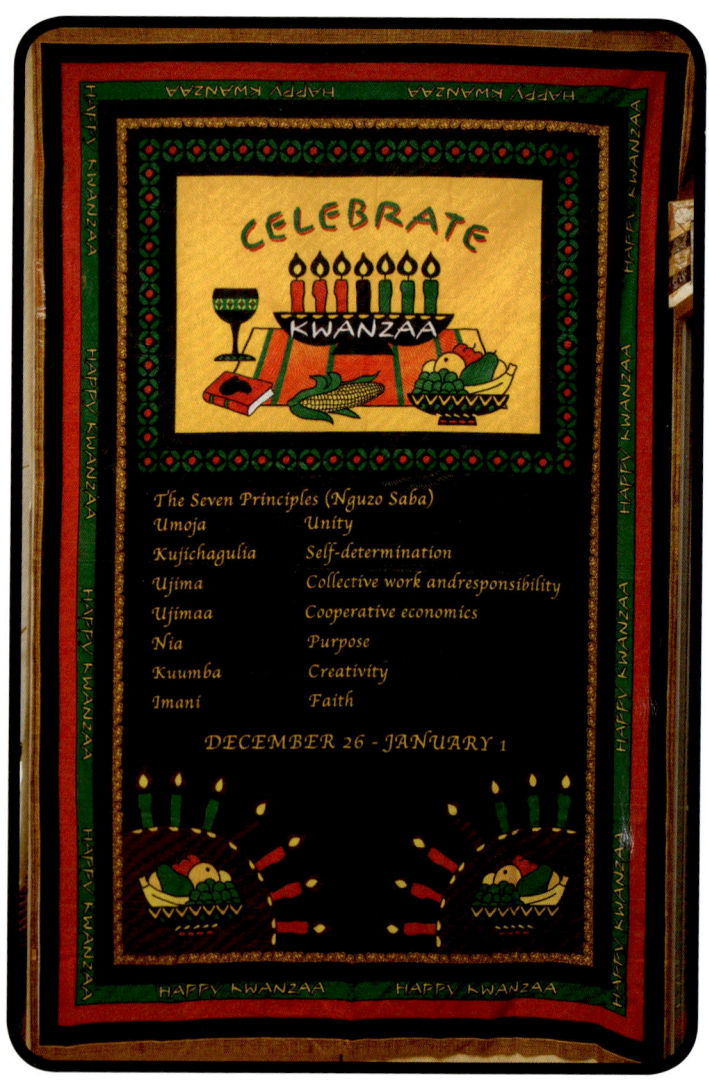

Kwanzaa's Nguzo Saba, or seven principles, include unity, purpose, and faith.

The Kwanzaa Set

The seven Kwanzaa symbols are:
 mkeka (m-KAY-kah), or mat
 mazao (mah-SAH-o), or fruits and vegetables
 kikombe cha umoja (kee-KOM-bay cha oo-MO-jah), or unity cup
 muhindi (moo-HEEN-dee), or corn
 kinara (kee-NAH-rah), or candleholder
 mishumaa saba (MEE-shoo-MAH-ah SAH-bah), or seven candles
 zawadi (sah-WAH-dee), or gifts

vegetables are for the harvest. They also represent the rewards of work well done.

Corn is a separate Kwanzaa symbol. It is a grain that grows in South Africa. Each corn kernel is a seed that can be planted to grow more corn. To Africans, children are like seeds. They are the future. Collect an ear of corn for each child in your family. People who do not have children add an ear of corn to the display, too. In Africa, everyone in the community raises the children.

The unity cup is another Kwanzaa symbol. Family members drink together from this cup. This is done as an offering to the ancestors.

Look for a special cup, such as one without handles. Many unity cups are made of wood or metals such as silver or pewter.

Make room for a candleholder called a *kinara*. Keep it in a spot away from the cornhusks and other items that can burn. Your candleholder should be made of wood and hold seven candles. You will need one black candle, three red candles, and three green candles. The black candle is placed in the center. It stands for Africans and African Americans. Put the red candles on the left.

The wooden Kwanzaa kinara holds seven representative candles.

Family gifts, or zawadi, are one of the seven Kwanzaa symbols. These gifts are not mandatory and are usually given to children only.

They stand for the struggles of daily living. The green candles go on the right. Their green color stands for future hopes. Red candles are lit before green ones. This is to show that hard work and struggle lead to a better future.

Zawadi are gifts. Family gifts are the final Kwanzaa symbol. They can be homemade. They can be useful, such as books. People usually give gifts made in Africa or bought from a store owned by African Americans. Wrap them in bright African colors.

Chapter 4

The Seven Days of Kwanzaa

Kwanzaa lasts for one week. There are many things to do and different things to think about on each day. At the end of the week, families join together for a feast. Here is a day-by-day schedule of how to celebrate Kwanzaa.

December 26

Today is the first day of Kwanzaa. Light the black candle in the kinara. "Habari Gani (Hah-BAH-ree GAH-nee)?" an adult will ask. "What's the news?" The response is "Umoja!" *Umoja* means unity.

Families, friends, and neighbors come together for Umoja night. In some communities, they meet at town centers, churches, or halls. Leaders and teachers make speeches.

African drummers mark time on their drums. One of the leaders shouts "Harambee (hah-RAHM-bay)!" *Harambee* is a cheer. It is a call to pull together. Raise your right hand. Open your fingers. Pull your hand down to your side and make a fist. Do this seven times. That is harambee. You are pulling together. Then everyone lights a candle. They make a wish for the New Year.

December 27

Today is the second day of Kwanzaa. Light a black and a red candle in the kinara. "Habari Gani?" The correct response is "Kujichagulia!" This means self-determination.

Everyone has his or her own way of doing things. Your attitudes and habits make up your lifestyle. The way you walk, talk, eat, and dress tells others who you are. Deciding what works best for you in your life is self-determination. Knowing what you like and dislike about your culture is also important.

During Kwanzaa, many people try out African clothing and hairstyles. What is African style? That depends. On special days in the West African country of Ghana, men and women drape woven cloth around themselves. Beads and other jewelry are worn on the body or braided into hair and clothes. Boys may wear *dashikis* (dah-SHEE-kees) or long loose shirts. Flat round hats called *kufis* (KOO-fees) may sit atop their heads. Some women wrap their heads with scarves called *geles* (GAY-lays). In Northern Africa, veils may be worn that cover the hair and face. Men there wear tight headpieces called turbans.

Braided hairstyles are common among black people worldwide. Tight rows of braids are called cornrows. Dreadlocks are another African hairstyle. They form when sections of hair are rolled up or left to tangle into stiff knots.

People gather at community centers during Kwanzaa.

December 28

Today is the third day of Kwanzaa. Light a black, red, and green candle in the kinara. "Habari Gani?" Today's response is "Ujima!" *Ujima* means collective work and responsibility.

For Ujima, families tackle household chores together, such as cleaning out a workroom or planning a spring garden. They may visit older relatives and help them clean or cook a meal. Some community centers offer classes for families. Health, safety, nutrition, and family games are topics that are taught.

Teenager Kenya Jordana James created *Blackgirl Magazine*. It is a good example of Ujima. Young black women all around the country read this magazine. They send in articles about themselves and the issues that are important in their lives. Similar online magazines and chat rooms allow children and teens to make friends and talk through problems.

December 29

Today is the fourth day of Kwanzaa. Light one black candle, two red candles, and one green candle in the

The Fabric of Kwanzaa

Kente is a type of cloth from the country of Ghana. It is made by sewing together long brightly colored strips of handwoven cotton. Shirts, pants, hats, dresses, and stoles made of kente are worn during Kwanzaa. The colors and designs woven into the cloth have special meanings.

kinara. "Habari Gani?" Today, we respond "Ujamaa!" *Ujamaa* means cooperative economics.

Money and wealth are the focus of this day. Families may save money all year to make a big purchase everyone will use, such as a couch, TV, or car. They shop at local stores where they know the owners. There are also Ujamaa websites on the Internet. They have links to businesses around the world that are owned by Africans and African Americans.

Big cities such as Chicago hold Ujamaa holiday markets. These are flea markets and arts and crafts fairs similar to the open-air markets found in African cities. African clothing, musical instruments, art, food, and handmade items are sold there. You will need to bargain to get the best price.

Sharing and being generous is another way to approach the

Vendors sell a variety of woven fabrics and other handmade African wares and foods at Ujamaa holiay markets throughout the Kwanzaa season.

day. Collecting food, clothing, and money for the poor is a rewarding Ujamaa activity. Some neighborhood groups try to think of ways to help out. They form carpools, babysitting clubs, and neighborhood watches. Others hold toy, book, tool, and jewelry swaps.

December 30

Today is the fifth day of Kwanzaa. Light one black candle, two red candles, and two green candles in the kinara. "Habari Gani?" People respond "Nia!" *Nia* means purpose.

When do you feel most alive? What do you do that brings joy to others? These are questions family members ask each other on this day. All around us there are examples of people who make a difference in our lives. How do you show your thanks?

A roll call to the ancestors is a Kwanzaa ceremony that honors personal and historical heroes. An adult will begin by naming an important African or African American.

Relatives who have passed away are also named. Anyone else who wants to may then name a hero and tell something about that person. How many famous African American men and women can you name?

December 31

Today is the sixth day of Kwanzaa. Light one black candle, three red candles, and two green candles in the kinara. "Habari Gani?" Today, we say "Kuumba!" *Kuumba* means creativity.

A *karuma* is a harvest feast. There are no set Kwanzaa menus, so families cook their own favorite recipes. Traditional Southern foods, such as greens, sweet potatoes, and fried chicken are often served. Creole dishes, such as a stew called jambalaya, and African foods, such as plantains and okra, might also be present. Try making an African chicken stew using the recipe on the next page. Hoppin' John, a southern dish made with black-eyed peas, is said to bring luck in the New Year.

Before the meal, an elder will pour water from the unity cup into a bowl of lettuce or greens. The elder will spill the water four times—one for each of the four directions: north, south, east, and west. Then, he or she will make a toast to the ancestors and drink from the cup. The cup is passed around the table and everyone takes a drink. This ceremony is called *tambiko* (tahm-BEE-koh).

Although food is central to the karuma, it is not the only party activity. There may be music and dancing. At the first Kwanzaa

Botswanan Chicken Groundnut Stew*

Ingredients:

1 chicken, cut into serving pieces
1 tablespoon vegetable oil
1 medium onion, chopped
1 bell pepper, chopped
1 cup water
½ cup peanut or almond butter
½ cup tomato paste
1 teaspoon ginger, grated
2 tablespoons brown sugar
½ teaspoon chili flakes
1 (15 oz) can tomatoes, diced

Directions:

1. Mix the peanut butter or almond butter, tomato paste, ginger, brown sugar, and chili flakes in a large bowl. These ingredients will make the sauce.
2. Slowly pour the water into these ingredients while continuously stirring with a whisk until the sauce is smooth.
3. Add the oil to a large frying pan on medium-high heat. Add the chicken pieces to the oil and sauté them until they begin to brown. Make sure your frying pan has a lid—you will need this later.
4. When the chicken begins to brown, add the onions and peppers. Keep sautéing until the chicken is brown all over and the onions are translucent.
5. Add the peanut sauce and the tomatoes to the chicken. Cover the pan and turn the heat down to low so the stew will simmer slowly. Continue to simmer for 45-60 minutes.
6. When the dish is almost done, taste the sauce and add salt if needed.
7. Serve the stew with rice or couscous.

* Adult supervision required.

celebration, seven children performed a Kwanzaa skit. Families also exchange Kwanzaa gifts.

January 1

Today is the seventh day of Kwanzaa. Light all of the candles in the kinara. "Habari Gani?" The final response is "Imani!" *Imani* means faith.

The last day of Kwanzaa is a day of meditation. When you meditate, you are quiet and thoughtful. You think about your life and how you can improve it. Some families reflect upon the changes in their lives over the past year. There might have been births, weddings, and funerals. People have moved away from or entered into the family. All these joyful and sad occasions are remembered.

All kinds of delicious foods are prepared for the Kwanzaa feast, or karuma. Long tables hold African, Creole, and southern fare.

24

Chapter 5

Celebrate Kwanzaa

Kwanzaa started out in 1966 as an informal holiday celebrated by one man and his friends and family. Over the years, it has grown into a much bigger event. From Africa to Canada, from Brazil to Barbados, people celebrate Kwanzaa.

Growing in Popularity

In the United States, schools nationwide hold Kwanzaa programs. They include Kwanzaa among the winter holidays they teach each year. Public libraries have special programs for Kwanzaa. Storytellers tell African American folktales, such as the Brer Rabbit stories. They also tell African folktales, such as those featuring Anansi the Spider. Children's museums and zoos offer Kwanzaa activities and exhibits.

Kwanzaa has become more popular as years have passed. You can watch Kwanzaa movies and animated TV specials. You can buy Kwanzaa sets, cards, baskets, dolls, and even Kwanzaa candy bars.

Museums, schools, and libraries offer programs for children to learn about and celebrate Kwanzaa.

In 1997, the United States Postal Service issued a Kwanzaa postage stamp.

A Wonderful Creation

In the United States, anyone can invent a holiday. We are free to celebrate whatever we like. Cinco de Mayo, St. Patrick's Day, and the Chinese New Year are other holidays that focus on just some of the many different cultures represented in our country. The First Amendment to the Constitution of the United States guarantees the right of any group to gather peacefully for any reason.

Kwanzaa is a holiday created by and for African Americans. But it is also a holiday about family values. The teachings of Kwanzaa encourage respect for people of all colors. Dr. Karenga believes that the message of Kwanzaa is universal. "Any message that is good for a particular people," he says, "speaks not just to that people. It speaks to the world."

Kwanzaa Craft*

Mancala is one of the oldest board games in the world. Most African tribes have their own special name for the game and their own ways of playing it. Today, mancala is popular all over the world. Like chess or checkers, it is a two-person game. You must think and plan ahead before you make a move. Play mancala with your family and friends during Kwanzaa!

Here are the supplies you will need:

- Empty egg carton
- 2 plastic containers
- 48 small game pieces, such as beads, seeds, pebbles, or marbles

Directions:

1. Remove the lid of the egg carton. The bottom half of the carton is the game board. There should be twelve egg cups in all.
2. Place four game pieces in each egg cup. Game pieces can be any small items that fit inside the egg cups.
3. Set a plastic container on both ends of the egg carton. These are the mancalas, or game piece bowls.
4. Each player has one row of six egg cups. The mancala, or game bowl, to the right of each player is his or her game piece bowl.

How to Play:

1. The first player takes all the game pieces out of one of his or her six egg cups. He or she must then drop a game piece into the next cups to his or her right, following the board in a counter-clockwise direction. Drop just one game piece into each cup. The amount of game pieces you have in your hand tells you how many cups you will drop pieces into. For example, if

Counting Game

there were four game pieces in the cup you chose, then you will place one game piece in each of the next four cups on the board.

The mancalas also count as the cups you must drop the game pieces into. Game pieces can be placed into your own mancala. But do not drop your game pieces into your opponent's mancala.

The second player will then remove all the game pieces from one of his or her egg cups. He or she must also place one game piece in each cup on the game board in a counter-clockwise direction.

The game continues until one player's egg cups are empty. When this happens, the other player removes all of the game pieces still in his or her egg cups and places them into his or her mancala.

Then both players count the number of game pieces in their mancalas. The player with the most game pieces wins the game.

ecial Kwanzaa rules: Any player who has seven game pieces in one of his or r egg cups may place all seven pieces in his or her mancala. Then he or she ay take another turn.

*Safety note: Be sure to ask for help from an adult, if needed, to complete this project.

Glossary

culture—The customs, beliefs, and ways of life of a group of people.

faith—For Kwanzaa, faith involves believing strongly in yourself, your abilities, and the community in which you live.

festival—A time of celebration.

harvest—Gathering of crops.

hemisphere—Half of a sphere or globe. The equator divides planet Earth into its northern and southern hemispheres.

heritage—Traditions or property from earlier generations of ancestors.

identity—Who a person is.

principles—Values that guide people's actions.

Swahili—An African language.

symbol—An object that represents or stands for an idea or thought.

Learn More

Books

Felix, Rebecca. *We Celebrate Kwanzaa in Winter.* Ann Arbor, MI: Cherry Lake Publishing, 2015.

Herrington, Lisa. *Kwanzaa.* New York, NY: Children's Press, 2014.

Pettiford, Rebecca. *Kwanzaa.* Minneapolis, MN: Bullfrog Books, 2015.

Rau, Dana Meachen. *Creating Winter Crafts.* Ann Arbor, MI: Cherry Lake Publishing, 2014.

Websites

DLTK's Kwanzaa Crafts for Kids
dltk-kids.com/crafts/kwanzaa/
Learn how to make amazing Kwanzaa crafts with regular household items.

Enchanted Learning's Kwanzaa Page
enchantedlearning.com/crafts/kwanza/
This site has great ideas for activities and crafts and plenty of Kwanzaa-related puzzles.

The Official Kwanzaa Website
officialkwanzaawebsite.org
Learn about the seven principles of Kwanzaa and how the holiday began.

Index

A
Africa, 5–7, 10–11, 13, 15, 18, 25
African Americans, 5–11, 14–15, 20–21, 25, 27
Anansi the Spider, 26

B
Barbados, 25
bendera, 6
Blackgirl Magazine, 19
Brazil, 25
Brer Rabbit, 25

C
California, 8
Canada, 25
Chicago, 20
children, 13, 19, 24, 26
Chinese New Year, 27
Christmas, 5
Cinco de Mayo, 27
civil rights, 9
Constitution, 27
corn, 13–14
culture, 8–9, 17, 27

D
dashikis, 18

F
faith, 11, 24
festival, 5, 7
first fruits, 7
food, 7, 20–22

G
geles, 18
Ghana, 17
gifts, 5, 15, 24

H
hair, 6, 17–18
harambee, 17
harvest, 5, 7, 13, 22
hemisphere, 5
heritage, 5
history, 8–9, 11
Hoppin' John, 22

I
identity, 9
Imani, 11, 24

J
jambalaya, 22
James, Kenya Jordana, 19

K
Karenga, Maulana, 7–11, 27
karuma, 22
kente, 19
kinara, 14, 16–18, 20–22, 24
kufis, 18
Kujichagulia, 11, 17
kuumba, 11, 22

M
mancala, 28–29
markets, 20
matunda ya kwanza, 7
mazao, 13
mkeka, 13

N
New Year's Day, 5, 17, 22, 24
Nguzo Saba, 11
Nia, 11, 21

O
okra, 22

P
plantains, 22
principles, 11

S
seven, 5, 11, 14, 17, 24
slavery, 9–10
St. Patrick's Day, 27
Swahili, 6–7
symbols, 12–13, 15

T
tambiko, 22
Thanksgiving, 7

U
Ujamaa, 11, 20–21
Ujima, 11, 18–19
Umoja, 11, 16
United States, 5, 7, 25, 27
United States Postal Service, 27
unity cup, 13–14, 22

V
values, 27

Z
zawadi, 15